PRINCEWILL LAGANG

The Mindful Entrepreneur: Balance in a Hectic World

First published by PRINCEWILL LAGANG 2023

Copyright © 2023 by Princewill Lagang

All rights reserved. No part of this publication may be reproduced, stored or transmitted in any form or by any means, electronic, mechanical, photocopying, recording, scanning, or otherwise without written permission from the publisher. It is illegal to copy this book, post it to a website, or distribute it by any other means without permission.

Princewill Lagang asserts the moral right to be identified as the author of this work.

First edition

This book was professionally typeset on Reedsy.
Find out more at reedsy.com

# Contents

1. The Mindful Entrepreneur: Balance in a Hectic World — 1
2. The Art of Mindful Awareness — 4
3. Mindful Leadership: Guiding with Presence and Purpose — 8
4. Mindful Decision-Making: Clarity in the Face of Complexity — 12
5. Work-Life Integration: A Mindful Approach to Balance — 16
6. Resilience and Mindfulness: Thriving in the Face of... — 20
7. Building a Purpose-Driven Business: Mindfulness and Social... — 24
8. Mindful Growth and Scaling: Balancing Expansion and... — 28
9. Mindful Adaptation and Innovation: Navigating Change in... — 32
10. Mindful Success: The Culmination of a Balanced... — 36
11. A Mindful Entrepreneur's Legacy: Nurturing the Next... — 40
12. Conclusion - The Endless Journey of Mindful Entrepreneurship — 43

# 1

# The Mindful Entrepreneur: Balance in a Hectic World

In a world that never seems to slow down, where the digital age has brought unparalleled opportunities and relentless demands, the concept of balance often feels like an elusive dream. Entrepreneurship, with its boundless potential for creativity, innovation, and financial success, has become a symbol of the modern business landscape. However, beneath the surface of glossy success stories and the allure of flexible schedules lies a reality that many entrepreneurs face: a constant juggling act, both personally and professionally.

For those who have ventured into the entrepreneurial realm, it's no secret that the path is riddled with obstacles and challenges. The typical day of an entrepreneur is a blend of exhilarating highs and exhausting lows, where triumphs and tribulations often overlap, leaving them navigating the turbulent waters of ambiguity. In this chaotic landscape, it's easy to get swept away by the never-ending to-do lists, the pressure to scale, and the drive to make a mark on the world. As a result, the very qualities that drove individuals to become entrepreneurs—passion, innovation, and determination—can become the same elements that threaten to consume them.

But what if there were a different way? What if, in the whirlwind of entrepreneurship, there was a path to not only succeed in business but also thrive in life? This book, "The Mindful Entrepreneur: Balance in a Hectic World," explores just that.

The Entrepreneurial Paradox

To understand the need for mindfulness in entrepreneurship, we must first acknowledge the paradox that entrepreneurs often find themselves in. On one hand, they are celebrated for their ability to create, innovate, and take calculated risks. On the other hand, they grapple with the immense pressure to continuously perform, deliver results, and adapt to an ever-changing business landscape.

Entrepreneurs are notorious for their go-getter attitude, relentless ambition, and a willingness to work long hours. But this mindset can lead to a detrimental work-life imbalance. The common notion of "hustle until you make it" can take a toll on one's mental and physical health, relationships, and overall quality of life.

In a world that celebrates non-stop hustle, the term "mindfulness" may seem out of place. Often associated with meditation, yoga, and Zen philosophy, mindfulness might appear at odds with the aggressive drive of entrepreneurship. But in reality, it's precisely this state of mind that can bring equilibrium to the hectic world of entrepreneurship.

The Power of Mindfulness

Mindfulness, at its core, is about cultivating awareness. It's the practice of being fully present in the moment, attuned to your thoughts, emotions, and physical sensations. This heightened state of awareness allows you to make better choices, manage stress, and create a sense of balance in your life.

For entrepreneurs, mindfulness isn't about slowing down or becoming passive; it's about finding clarity and focus amid the chaos. It's about being able to pivot and adapt without being overwhelmed. It's the key to making decisions that are aligned with your values and long-term goals, rather than being reactive and driven solely by immediate demands.

In this book, we will explore how mindfulness can help you thrive as an entrepreneur. You'll learn how to harness its power to enhance your creativity, make more informed decisions, build stronger relationships, and ultimately achieve a sense of equilibrium in a world that seems designed to disrupt it.

Over the following chapters, we'll delve into practical strategies, real-life case studies, and exercises to help you embrace mindfulness in your entrepreneurial journey. We'll explore how you can apply it to various aspects of your life, from managing stress and cultivating resilience to building a purpose-driven business that aligns with your values.

In the end, the mindful entrepreneur is not a contradiction in terms but a blueprint for success that is firmly rooted in the present moment, guided by a deep understanding of self and a clear vision for the future. It's about embracing the entrepreneurial spirit while nurturing your well-being, and finding the elusive balance that can make your journey both fulfilling and sustainable.

So, let's embark on this exploration together, as we discover the transformative potential of mindfulness in the dynamic world of entrepreneurship.

# 2

# The Art of Mindful Awareness

In the previous chapter, we introduced the concept of the mindful entrepreneur and explored the paradoxical nature of entrepreneurship. We recognized that the relentless pursuit of success and the constant demand for innovation can leave entrepreneurs feeling overwhelmed and out of balance. Mindfulness, with its emphasis on cultivating awareness and presence, offers a way to address these challenges. In this chapter, we'll dive deeper into the practice of mindfulness and examine how it can be a valuable tool for entrepreneurs seeking balance in a hectic world.

The Essence of Mindfulness

Mindfulness is often described as the art of paying attention to the present moment without judgment. It involves being fully engaged in what you are doing, whether it's a business meeting, a creative brainstorming session, or a simple moment of relaxation. Mindfulness is not about escaping from reality but rather about engaging with it more authentically.

At its core, mindfulness is an antidote to the autopilot mode that many of us find ourselves in. In our fast-paced world, it's easy to get caught up in a constant stream of thoughts, worries about the past or future, and distractions from our devices. This scattered mental state can leave us feeling overwhelmed, stressed, and disconnected from the experiences that matter most.

As an entrepreneur, the ability to remain fully present and attentive is a game-changer. It allows you to make more informed decisions, build stronger relationships, and unlock your creativity. Mindfulness helps you break free from the constraints of reactivity and empowers you to respond to challenges with poise and clarity.

The Benefits of Mindful Awareness

To fully appreciate the value of mindfulness for entrepreneurs, let's explore some of its key benefits:

1. Stress Reduction: Mindfulness has been scientifically proven to reduce stress levels. In the high-stakes world of entrepreneurship, stress is a constant companion. Mindful awareness can help you manage stress, enabling you to make clearer decisions and maintain your well-being.

2. Enhanced Creativity: When your mind is cluttered with worries and distractions, it can be challenging to tap into your creative potential. Mindfulness can help clear the mental clutter, making space for innovative ideas and solutions.

3. Improved Decision-Making: Entrepreneurs are constantly faced with decisions, big and small. Mindfulness allows you to make decisions with greater insight and a heightened awareness of your goals and values.

4. Resilience Building: Entrepreneurship is fraught with setbacks and failures. Mindful awareness helps you develop resilience, enabling you to bounce back from challenges with greater ease.

5. Better Relationships: Whether it's with employees, partners, or customers, strong relationships are essential for business success. Mindfulness fosters better communication, active listening, and empathy, all of which are vital for building positive connections.

6. Alignment with Values: Mindfulness helps you stay aligned with your core values and long-term vision. It ensures that your business decisions are in harmony with your personal principles.

Practical Techniques for Mindful Awareness

To begin your journey into mindfulness, you can start with some simple techniques that can be incorporated into your daily routine. Here are a few practices to get you started:

1. Mindful Breathing: Take a few moments each day to focus on your breath. Notice the sensation of the breath entering and leaving your body. This simple practice can help calm your mind and ground you in the present moment.

2. Mindful Eating: Pay close attention to the sensory experience of eating. Savor the flavors, textures, and smells of your food. This practice can be a powerful way to bring mindfulness into your daily life.

3. Body Scan: Spend a few minutes scanning your body from head to toe, noting any areas of tension or discomfort. This practice can help you become more attuned to physical sensations and promote relaxation.

4. Meditation: Consider incorporating meditation into your routine. Even just a few minutes a day can have a profound impact on your mindfulness practice. There are various meditation apps and guided sessions available to get you started.

In the chapters that follow, we'll explore how you can apply mindfulness to specific aspects of entrepreneurship, from leadership and decision-making to work-life balance and managing adversity. As you embrace the art of mindful awareness, you'll discover the transformative power it holds for creating a more balanced and fulfilling entrepreneurial journey.

# 3

# Mindful Leadership: Guiding with Presence and Purpose

In our exploration of mindfulness and its application in the entrepreneurial world, we have begun to understand the significance of cultivating awareness and presence in our daily lives. As we delve deeper into this journey, it becomes increasingly important to consider the role of mindful leadership in entrepreneurship. Leadership, whether you're leading a startup, a team, or an entire organization, is a central aspect of entrepreneurship, and it's an area where mindfulness can make a profound difference.

The Mindful Leader's Paradigm

A mindful leader is one who leads with presence and purpose. Mindful leadership is about creating a work environment that fosters well-being, engagement, and growth. It's a shift from the conventional authoritarian or transactional leadership styles to a more transformative, people-centered approach.

Here are some key characteristics of a mindful leader:

1. Self-Awareness: Mindful leaders are acutely aware of their own strengths, weaknesses, and emotional triggers. They understand the impact of their actions on others.

2. Empathy: They exhibit deep empathy and understanding toward their team members. They appreciate the unique strengths and challenges of each individual.

3. Active Listening: Mindful leaders are exceptional listeners. They give their full attention to what others are saying without interrupting or judging. This encourages open communication and trust.

4. Resilience: They are adept at handling stress and adversity, setting an example for their team. Their resilience serves as a source of inspiration during challenging times.

5. Clear Communication: Mindful leaders communicate with clarity and transparency, ensuring that their team members understand the organization's goals and values.

6. Decisiveness: While mindful leaders value input and feedback, they are also capable of making decisive and timely decisions.

Mindful Leadership in Action

As an entrepreneur, you might be wondering how to embody mindful leadership in your own venture. Here are some practical steps you can take:

1. Self-Reflection: Begin by cultivating self-awareness. Reflect on your leadership style, your strengths, and areas where you can improve. Journaling can be a helpful tool for this process.

2. Active Listening: Practice active listening with your team. When someone speaks, focus on their words and non-verbal cues. Encourage open and honest communication within your organization.

3. Empathy: Show empathy toward your team members. Understand their challenges, aspirations, and perspectives. Empathy fosters a culture of support and trust.

4. Mindful Decision-Making: Before making important decisions, take a moment to center yourself. Consider the potential impact on your team, your customers, and your business as a whole.

5. Conflict Resolution: When conflicts arise, approach them with a calm and open mindset. Seek resolutions that consider the well-being of all parties involved.

6. Cultivate Resilience: Develop your own resilience through mindfulness practices. This will not only benefit your leadership but also inspire your team to be more resilient in the face of adversity.

7. Lead by Example: Be the embodiment of the values and principles you want your team to uphold. Your actions will set the tone for your organization's culture.

Mindful Leadership and Business Success

Mindful leadership is not just a philosophical approach to leadership; it has practical implications for business success. When you lead with mindfulness, you create a workplace that is more inclusive, engaged, and innovative. Here are some of the tangible benefits:

1. Higher Employee Satisfaction: Mindful leadership leads to a more positive workplace culture, which, in turn, results in higher job satisfaction among

employees.

2. Enhanced Creativity: A mindful leader encourages open dialogue and the sharing of ideas, fostering a culture of innovation and creativity.

3. Improved Decision-Making: Mindful leaders are better equipped to make informed and balanced decisions that benefit the organization in the long term.

4. Reduced Turnover: A positive workplace culture and strong leadership can reduce employee turnover, saving time and resources in recruitment and training.

5. Increased Productivity: Employees are more likely to be productive and motivated when they feel valued and heard by their leaders.

As we move forward in our exploration of mindfulness in entrepreneurship, keep in mind that mindful leadership is not just about the "soft skills" of leadership. It's a strategic approach that can lead to tangible business success while also creating a more meaningful and balanced entrepreneurial journey. In the chapters that follow, we'll continue to delve into how mindfulness can be applied to various aspects of entrepreneurship, from decision-making to work-life balance, helping you create a thriving business and a fulfilling life.

# 4

# Mindful Decision-Making: Clarity in the Face of Complexity

Entrepreneurship is a constant stream of decisions, both big and small. From strategic choices that shape the direction of your business to daily operational decisions, your ability to make informed, balanced, and effective decisions is critical to your success. In this chapter, we'll explore how mindfulness can enhance your decision-making process, helping you navigate the complexities of entrepreneurship with clarity and confidence.

The Decision-Making Challenge

Entrepreneurs often face a unique set of challenges when making decisions. The pressure to innovate, compete, and adapt to rapidly changing markets can make decision-making feel like a high-stakes game. In this environment, it's easy to succumb to decision fatigue, rush into choices without sufficient analysis, or become paralyzed by the fear of making the wrong decision.

Moreover, the emotional rollercoaster that often accompanies entrepreneurship, with its ups and downs, can cloud judgment. Decisions made in the heat of the moment can have far-reaching consequences, both positive and negative.

The Role of Mindfulness in Decision-Making

Mindfulness equips entrepreneurs with a valuable set of tools for navigating the decision-making process. Here's how it can help:

1. Clarity of Thought: Mindfulness helps clear the mental clutter. By being fully present in the moment, you can assess the situation objectively, free from emotional bias or racing thoughts.

2. Emotional Regulation: Mindfulness enables you to manage the emotional ups and downs of entrepreneurship, reducing the risk of impulsive decisions driven by fear, frustration, or anxiety.

3. Focused Attention: It allows you to focus on the relevant information and considerations, filtering out distractions and irrelevant data that can cloud judgment.

4. Enhanced Intuition: Mindfulness can sharpen your intuition, helping you trust your gut feelings when making decisions, especially in situations where information is limited.

5. Balanced Perspective: It encourages you to see the bigger picture and consider the long-term consequences of your decisions, ensuring they align with your business goals and values.

Practical Mindful Decision-Making Techniques

To apply mindfulness to your decision-making process, consider these techniques:

1. Mindful Pause: Before making a decision, take a moment to pause. Breathe deeply and observe your thoughts and emotions. This brief mindfulness practice can help you detach from the heat of the moment and gain clarity.

2. Stakeholder Mapping: Consider the impact of your decision on various stakeholders, including employees, customers, and partners. This can help you make decisions that are balanced and considerate of all interests.

3. Pros and Cons Analysis: Use a structured approach to weigh the pros and cons of different options. Mindfulness can help you approach this analysis with a clear and calm mind.

4. Scenario Visualization: Imagine the potential outcomes of your decisions. This can help you anticipate challenges and opportunities, making it easier to make informed choices.

5. Consultation: Seek input from trusted advisors, mentors, or colleagues. Mindfully listen to their perspectives and use their insights to inform your decision.

6. Post-Decision Reflection: After making a decision, take time to reflect on the process and the outcome. What did you learn from the experience? How can you apply this knowledge to future decisions?

A Balanced Approach to Risk

Entrepreneurship inherently involves risk-taking. Mindfulness does not eliminate risk but equips you to take calculated and balanced risks. It helps you differentiate between reckless impulsivity and informed risk-taking by providing a clear and steady mindset.

In the ever-evolving landscape of entrepreneurship, mastering the art of mindful decision-making is a valuable skill that can set you apart as an entrepreneur. It enables you to embrace uncertainty with confidence, make choices that resonate with your values, and ultimately, steer your business toward success.

As we continue our exploration of mindfulness in entrepreneurship, we'll delve into other crucial aspects, including work-life balance, building resilience, and managing adversity. These insights and practices will provide you with a holistic toolkit for creating a thriving business while nurturing a balanced and fulfilling life.

# 5

# Work-Life Integration: A Mindful Approach to Balance

The pursuit of entrepreneurship often comes with a relentless work ethic and a blurred line between personal and professional life. Entrepreneurs frequently find themselves juggling multiple roles, facing intense workloads, and wrestling with the pressure to succeed. In this chapter, we'll explore the importance of work-life integration in entrepreneurship and how mindfulness can play a crucial role in achieving balance.

The Work-Life Dilemma

For many entrepreneurs, work and life are often seen as two separate, competing entities. The struggle to balance the demands of building and running a business with personal life can lead to burnout, strained relationships, and a diminished quality of life. The pursuit of success sometimes comes at the cost of well-being.

The traditional concept of "work-life balance" implies a strict division between work and personal life, where one should not encroach upon the other. In reality, this strict separation can be challenging to maintain for entrepreneurs, whose work is often intertwined with their identity and passion. Instead of balance, work-life integration allows for a more flexible and sustainable approach.

Work-Life Integration with Mindfulness

Work-life integration, guided by mindfulness, acknowledges that personal and professional life are not mutually exclusive but interconnected. Mindfulness helps entrepreneurs create a more harmonious and flexible relationship between the two. Here's how:

1. Present Moment Awareness: Mindfulness encourages you to be fully present, whether you're working on a project or spending time with loved ones. This enhances the quality of both your work and personal life.

2. Setting Boundaries: Mindfulness helps you establish clear boundaries, allowing you to focus on work when necessary and fully engage in personal life without work-related distractions.

3. Prioritization: Mindfulness helps you identify and prioritize what truly matters in both work and personal life, ensuring that your actions align with your values.

4. Stress Reduction: By managing stress through mindfulness practices, you can prevent the negative spillover of work-related stress into your personal life.

5. Self-Care: Mindfulness encourages self-care practices, which are essential for maintaining well-being and sustaining your entrepreneurial journey.

Practical Tips for Work-Life Integration

To integrate work and life mindfully, consider these practical tips:

1. Set Clear Boundaries: Define specific work hours and designate a separate workspace at home. When your workday ends, close the door (literally or metaphorically) to signify the transition.

2. Prioritize Self-Care: Make self-care a non-negotiable part of your routine. This includes exercise, meditation, healthy eating, and quality sleep. A healthy you is a more effective entrepreneur.

3. Mindful Transitions: Create rituals to transition between work and personal life. This can be as simple as taking a few deep breaths or going for a short walk to clear your mind.

4. Family and Friends: Set aside dedicated time for family and friends. Be fully present with them, even if it's for a short period. Quality matters more than quantity.

5. Unplugged Time: Establish screen-free time for yourself and your loved ones. Disconnect from emails, notifications, and devices to truly be present.

6. Delegate and Outsource: Don't hesitate to delegate tasks or outsource aspects of your business that can be handled by others. This frees up your time and reduces stress.

The Benefits of Work-Life Integration

Mindful work-life integration provides several advantages for entrepreneurs:

1. Improved Well-Being: Balancing work and personal life promotes mental and physical well-being, reducing stress and preventing burnout.

2. Enhanced Productivity: By fostering a healthier work environment and

mindset, you become more productive and creative in your entrepreneurial endeavors.

3. Stronger Relationships: Building and maintaining meaningful connections with loved ones becomes easier when you're fully present in your personal life.

4. Sustainability: Mindful work-life integration ensures that your entrepreneurial journey remains sustainable in the long run, as you're more likely to enjoy the process.

5. Greater Fulfillment: Striking a balance between work and life allows you to find greater fulfillment in both, enriching your overall experience.

As you continue your journey as a mindful entrepreneur, remember that work-life integration is an ongoing practice. It requires constant self-reflection, adjustment, and fine-tuning to ensure that both your professional and personal life align with your values and well-being. In the chapters that follow, we'll delve into other critical aspects of entrepreneurship, including building resilience, managing adversity, and creating a purpose-driven business that reflects your mindful approach.

# 6

# Resilience and Mindfulness: Thriving in the Face of Adversity

Entrepreneurship is a journey filled with challenges, setbacks, and unexpected twists. In these turbulent waters, resilience is a quality that can make all the difference between giving up and pushing forward. This chapter explores the intersection of mindfulness and resilience, and how these two powerful attributes can help you not just survive but thrive in the face of adversity.

The Resilience Imperative

Resilience is the ability to bounce back from setbacks, adapt to change, and thrive despite adversity. It's a crucial trait for entrepreneurs, as the entrepreneurial path is often riddled with uncertainty, failure, and unforeseen obstacles. A resilient entrepreneur is not only able to weather the storms but can emerge stronger and more determined.

Mindfulness and Resilience

Mindfulness and resilience are closely linked. Mindfulness practices, which encourage staying present in the moment, help you develop a more robust and adaptable mindset. Here's how mindfulness contributes to resilience:

1. Emotional Regulation: Mindfulness teaches you to observe your emotions without judgment. This emotional regulation can help you stay calm and composed when faced with adversity.

2. Stress Management: Mindfulness equips you with effective stress management tools, allowing you to navigate high-stress situations more gracefully.

3. Adaptive Thinking: By being mindful of your thought patterns, you can identify and change negative or self-defeating beliefs, fostering a more optimistic and adaptive mindset.

4. Increased Focus: Mindfulness helps you stay focused on the task at hand, preventing distractions and enhancing problem-solving skills.

5. Self-Compassion: It encourages self-compassion, which is vital during challenging times. Being kind to yourself when things go wrong can help you bounce back more effectively.

Practical Steps to Build Resilience Through Mindfulness

Here are some practical steps you can take to build resilience through mindfulness:

1. Mindful Breathing: During difficult moments, pause and take a few mindful breaths. This can help you regain your composure and think more clearly.

2. Adversity as Opportunity: Practice viewing adversity as an opportunity

for growth and learning rather than a failure. A mindful perspective can transform challenges into stepping stones.

3. Gratitude Practice: Regularly express gratitude for the positive aspects of your life. This can provide a sense of perspective and balance during tough times.

4. Daily Mindfulness Ritual: Incorporate a daily mindfulness ritual into your routine, such as meditation or yoga. These practices can help you develop the mindfulness muscle.

5. Reflect on Past Successes: Recall past instances when you faced adversity and overcame it. This reflection can boost your self-confidence and resilience.

6. Build a Support System: Mindfulness also involves reaching out to others. Connect with mentors, friends, or a support network that can provide guidance and emotional support during challenging periods.

The Resilience Loop

Resilience and mindfulness form a powerful loop. The more you practice mindfulness, the more resilient you become. And as you build resilience, you become better equipped to stay mindful and focused during adversity. This feedback loop can help you thrive in the face of challenges and setbacks.

The Importance of Self-Compassion

Entrepreneurship often comes with a heavy burden of self-criticism. As you strive for success, it's easy to be harsh on yourself when things don't go as planned. Mindfulness emphasizes self-compassion, encouraging you to treat yourself with the same kindness and understanding you'd offer a friend facing a similar challenge.

Remember that resilience is not about suppressing negative emotions or ignoring difficulties. It's about acknowledging them, learning from them, and using them as a catalyst for personal and professional growth.

As you continue your journey as a mindful entrepreneur, resilience will become a valuable ally in your pursuit of success. By combining the power of mindfulness with the ability to bounce back from adversity, you'll not only endure the inevitable challenges of entrepreneurship but also use them as stepping stones to greater achievement. In the chapters that follow, we'll explore how to infuse mindfulness into various aspects of your business, including building a purpose-driven enterprise that aligns with your values.

# 7

# Building a Purpose-Driven Business: Mindfulness and Social Impact

Entrepreneurship is not just about creating financial success but also about making a positive impact on the world. In this chapter, we explore the concept of a purpose-driven business and how mindfulness can help entrepreneurs infuse their ventures with meaning and social significance.

The Quest for Meaning

Entrepreneurs often embark on their journey seeking more than just profit. They aspire to create a business that reflects their values, addresses societal issues, and contributes to positive change. This quest for meaning is at the heart of a purpose-driven business.

A purpose-driven business is one that prioritizes a mission beyond profit, striving to make a meaningful impact on society or the environment. It's a commitment to values and a vision for a better world.

Mindfulness and Purpose-Driven Entrepreneurship

Mindfulness plays a crucial role in the development of a purpose-driven business:

1. Clarity of Values: Mindfulness helps you gain clarity on your core values and beliefs. This self-awareness forms the foundation of a purpose-driven venture, ensuring that your business aligns with what truly matters to you.

2. Social Responsibility: Mindfulness encourages a sense of responsibility toward the greater good. It guides you to consider the societal and environmental impact of your business decisions.

3. Sustainable Practices: A mindful entrepreneur is more likely to implement sustainable and ethical practices, ensuring that the business is aligned with its purpose.

4. Compassion: Mindfulness fosters compassion, which is vital for understanding the needs and challenges of others. This empathy can guide the direction of your purpose-driven business.

Practical Steps to Create a Purpose-Driven Business

Here are practical steps to infuse mindfulness into the process of creating a purpose-driven business:

1. Define Your Purpose: Clearly articulate your business's purpose and mission. What positive change do you want to bring to the world? How will your business contribute to this change?

2. Integrate Mindfulness: Develop a mindfulness practice within your business culture. This can include mindfulness training for employees, meditation breaks, or the incorporation of mindful values into your company's mission

statement.

3. Sustainable Practices: Ensure that your business operates in an environmentally and socially responsible manner. Implement sustainable practices and consider the impact of your supply chain on the environment and local communities.

4. Stakeholder Engagement: Engage with stakeholders, including employees, customers, and partners, to align your business with their values and needs. Actively listen to their feedback and integrate it into your business strategy.

5. Transparency: Be transparent about your business practices and their impact. Transparency builds trust with your stakeholders and helps you live up to your purpose-driven mission.

6. Measure Impact: Develop metrics and key performance indicators to measure the impact of your purpose-driven efforts. Regularly assess and report on the progress you're making toward your mission.

The Benefits of a Purpose-Driven Business

Creating a purpose-driven business is not only fulfilling but also beneficial for your bottom line. Here are some of the advantages:

1. Attracting and Retaining Talent: Purpose-driven businesses often find it easier to attract and retain passionate and engaged employees who are aligned with the mission.

2. Customer Loyalty: Customers are increasingly drawn to businesses that prioritize social and environmental responsibility. Your purpose-driven mission can foster customer loyalty and trust.

3. Competitive Advantage: A well-defined purpose can set your business

apart from competitors, providing a unique selling proposition that resonates with a growing segment of conscious consumers.

4. Innovation and Creativity: A higher purpose can inspire innovation and creativity within your business, as employees are motivated by a meaningful mission.

5. Positive Impact: Most importantly, a purpose-driven business allows you to create a positive impact on society or the environment, contributing to a better world.

As a mindful entrepreneur, you have the unique opportunity to lead a business that not only succeeds financially but also thrives as a force for good. By integrating mindfulness into the core of your purpose-driven venture, you can make a lasting and positive impact on the world while achieving your entrepreneurial goals. In the chapters that follow, we'll continue our exploration of mindfulness in entrepreneurship, covering topics like effective leadership, decision-making, and work-life balance.

# 8

# Mindful Growth and Scaling: Balancing Expansion and Well-Being

Entrepreneurs often strive for growth and expansion, aiming to take their ventures to new heights. While business growth can bring opportunities and rewards, it can also pose challenges to maintaining a balanced and mindful approach. In this chapter, we'll explore the concept of mindful growth and scaling, emphasizing the importance of balancing expansion with well-being and purpose.

The Allure of Growth

The pursuit of growth is a fundamental driver for entrepreneurs. It can bring financial success, market recognition, and the satisfaction of seeing your vision materialize. However, unchecked and relentless growth can come at the cost of well-being, values, and the very purpose that inspired your entrepreneurial journey.

The Dilemma of Scaling Mindfully

# MINDFUL GROWTH AND SCALING: BALANCING EXPANSION AND...

Scaling a business mindfully means expanding with a focus on values, sustainability, and well-being, rather than just chasing bigger numbers. It's about achieving growth while preserving the essence of your purpose-driven mission and maintaining a harmonious work-life balance.

The Mindful Scaling Approach

Here are some key principles for mindful growth and scaling:

1. Reflect on Your Why: As you consider scaling your business, reflect on the core purpose that drives you. Ensure that growth aligns with your values and the positive impact you seek to create.

2. Prioritize Well-Being: Recognize that growth should not come at the expense of your well-being or the well-being of your team. Create a work environment that values mental and physical health.

3. Sustainable Practices: Implement sustainable and ethical business practices as you grow. This includes environmental responsibility, fair labor practices, and a commitment to social impact.

4. Leadership Development: Invest in the development of your leadership team to ensure that your company culture remains true to its values and mission as it expands.

5. Adapt and Innovate: Be open to adapting your business model and strategies as you scale. Innovation should be a core value that drives sustainable growth.

6. Stakeholder Engagement: Involve key stakeholders, including employees and customers, in the growth process. Their input can help you navigate expansion while maintaining alignment with your mission.

## The Benefits of Mindful Growth

Mindful growth and scaling offer several benefits for entrepreneurs and their businesses:

1. Long-Term Sustainability: Scaling mindfully ensures that your business remains viable and sustainable in the long term, avoiding overreaching and burnout.

2. Enhanced Reputation: Ethical and sustainable practices in your business contribute to a positive reputation, attracting customers who align with your values.

3. Employee Satisfaction: A workplace that prioritizes well-being and values-driven practices is more likely to attract and retain engaged and motivated employees.

4. Resilience: A business that grows with mindfulness is more adaptable and resilient in the face of challenges and changing market dynamics.

5. Alignment with Purpose: Mindful growth helps you stay connected with your original purpose and mission, ensuring that your business continues to make a positive impact.

## Balancing Growth and Mindfulness

Balancing growth and mindfulness requires ongoing reflection, self-awareness, and a commitment to maintaining your values and well-being as your business expands. It's an approach that prioritizes the journey as much as the destination, striving for success while staying true to your vision and mission.

As a mindful entrepreneur, you have the capacity to create a flourishing business that not only thrives financially but also aligns with your values and purpose. In the chapters that follow, we'll continue our exploration of mindfulness in entrepreneurship, covering topics such as effective leadership, decision-making, and work-life balance, providing you with a comprehensive toolkit for a fulfilling and balanced entrepreneurial journey.

# 9

# Mindful Adaptation and Innovation: Navigating Change in Business

In the dynamic world of entrepreneurship, change is the only constant. Successful entrepreneurs are not only adept at embracing change but also excel at innovating and adapting to evolving circumstances. In this chapter, we'll explore the vital role of mindfulness in adaptation and innovation, providing you with insights and strategies for navigating change in your business.

The Reality of Change

The business landscape is constantly evolving, driven by technological advancements, market shifts, and unforeseen disruptions. As an entrepreneur, you must be prepared to navigate these changes effectively to ensure the success and sustainability of your venture.

The Mindful Approach to Change

Mindfulness, with its focus on being present in the moment and maintaining a clear, non-reactive mindset, is a powerful tool for adapting to change. Here's how mindfulness contributes to successful adaptation and innovation:

1. Resilience: Mindfulness practices help you develop resilience, making it easier to bounce back from setbacks and adapt to unexpected challenges.

2. Creative Problem-Solving: A mindful mindset encourages creative and innovative problem-solving. By staying present and focused, you can discover new solutions to emerging issues.

3. Emotional Regulation: Mindfulness equips you to manage the emotional impact of change, helping you make decisions based on rational thinking rather than impulsive reactions.

4. Enhanced Communication: Effective adaptation often involves collaboration and communication with your team. Mindfulness improves your communication skills, promoting cooperation during transitions.

5. Stress Reduction: By managing stress through mindfulness practices, you can prevent the negative impact of change-related stress on your well-being and decision-making.

Practical Steps for Mindful Adaptation and Innovation

Here are practical steps to infuse mindfulness into your adaptation and innovation strategies:

1. Regular Mindfulness Practice: Consistently engage in mindfulness practices such as meditation or mindful breathing. These practices enhance your ability to stay present and focused during times of change.

2. Mindful Problem-Solving: Approach challenges with a problem-solving mindset informed by mindfulness. Take time to reflect on the issue at hand,

gather information, and think creatively about potential solutions.

3. Open Communication: Foster open and honest communication within your team. Encourage team members to share their insights and concerns, and be an active, mindful listener.

4. Mindful Decision-Making: When faced with important decisions during times of change, take a moment to center yourself and approach the decision with a calm and focused mindset.

5. Adaptive Leadership: As a leader, demonstrate flexibility and adaptability. Encourage your team to embrace change by setting an example of a mindful and open approach to adaptation.

The Benefits of Mindful Adaptation and Innovation

Embracing mindfulness in the face of change offers several benefits:

1. Enhanced Problem-Solving: Mindful adaptation and innovation lead to more effective problem-solving, helping you navigate change with greater ease and success.

2. Improved Resilience: By incorporating mindfulness into your response to change, you build resilience that allows you to bounce back from setbacks more quickly.

3. Innovation and Creativity: A mindful mindset encourages innovation and creativity, driving your business to find novel and effective solutions to challenges.

4. Stronger Team Collaboration: When your team adopts a mindful approach to change, it fosters stronger collaboration and communication, enhancing overall adaptability.

5. Better Well-Being: Mindful adaptation helps reduce the negative impact of stress, preserving your well-being during times of change.

As an entrepreneur, your ability to adapt and innovate in the face of change is a key determinant of your success. Mindfulness provides you with a powerful toolkit to navigate these changes with poise, creativity, and resilience. In the chapters that follow, we'll continue to explore how mindfulness can be applied to various aspects of entrepreneurship, including effective leadership, decision-making, and work-life balance, helping you build a thriving and balanced venture.

# 10

# Mindful Success: The Culmination of a Balanced Entrepreneurial Journey

In our exploration of mindfulness in entrepreneurship, we've delved into various aspects of building a successful and fulfilling venture. Now, we arrive at the culmination of this journey—the realization of mindful success. This chapter encapsulates the essence of a balanced entrepreneurial path and offers insights on how mindfulness can help you achieve success while nurturing well-being and purpose.

Defining Mindful Success

Mindful success goes beyond financial achievement; it encompasses well-being, purpose, and a harmonious balance between personal and professional life. It's about creating a venture that thrives in alignment with your values, mission, and a positive impact on the world.

Key Elements of Mindful Success

1. Alignment with Values: Mindful success begins with knowing your core

values and ensuring that your business decisions and actions align with them.

2. Purpose-Driven: A successful venture is driven by a clear and meaningful purpose that resonates with both you and your stakeholders.

3. Well-Being: Mindful success prioritizes the well-being of yourself, your team, and all those impacted by your business, fostering a positive and supportive work environment.

4. Adaptability and Innovation: Successful ventures are agile, adaptable, and open to innovation. Mindful entrepreneurs embrace change as an opportunity for growth.

5. Balance: Achieving balance in work and personal life is a hallmark of mindful success. It ensures that success is not a trade-off for well-being.

Principles of Mindful Success

To achieve mindful success, consider the following principles:

1. Continuous Learning: Be open to learning and personal growth. Success involves ongoing self-improvement and development.

2. Effective Leadership: Lead with authenticity, empathy, and a commitment to the well-being of your team.

3. Innovation and Adaptation: Embrace change as an opportunity to innovate and adapt your business to evolving circumstances.

4. Resilience: Cultivate resilience to bounce back from setbacks and persevere during challenging times.

5. Social Impact: Measure success not only by financial gains but also by the

positive impact your business makes on society and the environment.

6. Holistic Growth: Pursue holistic growth that encompasses both personal and professional development, fostering a well-rounded and balanced life.

Practical Steps for Mindful Success

Here are practical steps to integrate mindfulness into your journey towards success:

1. Regular Mindfulness Practice: Continue your regular mindfulness practice, as it is the foundation for maintaining mindfulness in all aspects of your entrepreneurial journey.

2. Reflect and Adjust: Periodically reflect on your progress and assess whether your business aligns with your values and purpose. Make necessary adjustments to realign when needed.

3. Seek Support: Build a support network of mentors, advisors, and peers who can provide guidance and insights as you strive for success.

4. Measure Impact: Develop clear metrics to measure the impact of your business on its stakeholders, the community, and the environment. Regularly review and assess these metrics.

5. Foster a Culture of Well-Being: Create a company culture that values the well-being of your team. Implement well-being initiatives and encourage a healthy work-life balance.

The Ongoing Journey of Mindful Success

Mindful success is an ongoing journey, not a destination. It is a path that continually evolves as you and your business grow. By embracing mindfulness as a guiding principle throughout your entrepreneurial journey, you can build a venture that thrives in alignment with your values and purpose, making a lasting impact on the world while nurturing your own well-being and fulfillment.

As you move forward, remember that success is not a singular achievement but a holistic pursuit that encompasses various aspects of your life and business. In this final chapter, we celebrate the culmination of your mindful entrepreneurial journey and encourage you to continue your quest for success in harmony with your values and well-being.

# 11

# A Mindful Entrepreneur's Legacy: Nurturing the Next Generation

As a mindful entrepreneur who has achieved success, you have the opportunity to leave a lasting legacy that extends beyond your business accomplishments. In this chapter, we explore the concept of legacy and how you can use your experience, knowledge, and resources to nurture the next generation of entrepreneurs and make a positive impact on the world.

Defining Your Legacy

Your legacy is the mark you leave on the world, the values you instill in others, and the impact you make beyond your own lifetime. It's a reflection of your values, beliefs, and the contributions you've made to society.

The Power of Mentorship

One of the most meaningful ways to create a legacy as a mindful entrepreneur is through mentorship. Sharing your knowledge, experience, and insights with aspiring entrepreneurs can have a profound impact on their journey and the future of entrepreneurship as a whole.

Mentorship benefits both you and your mentees:

1. Personal Fulfillment: Mentoring can be personally rewarding as you see your guidance and support making a difference in someone else's life.

2. Knowledge Transfer: You pass on your expertise and insights, helping the next generation of entrepreneurs avoid common pitfalls and make informed decisions.

3. Building a Supportive Network: Mentorship fosters a strong and supportive entrepreneurial community, where mentor and mentee relationships can turn into lifelong connections.

4. Creating a Legacy: By nurturing the growth and success of your mentees, you contribute to a positive and lasting legacy in the entrepreneurial world.

Practical Steps for Nurturing the Next Generation

Here are practical steps to create a legacy through mentorship:

1. Identify Your Mentees: Seek out aspiring entrepreneurs or individuals who can benefit from your guidance. They may be young professionals, students, or anyone with a passion for entrepreneurship.

2. Set Clear Expectations: Establish clear goals and expectations for the mentorship relationship. Define what you can offer and what your mentees hope to achieve.

3. Listen Actively: Act as an attentive and empathetic listener. Understand your mentees' goals, challenges, and aspirations.

4. Share Knowledge and Insights: Provide guidance, share your experiences, and offer valuable insights. Help your mentees make informed decisions.

5. Encourage Growth: Support your mentees in their personal and professional growth. Encourage them to take risks, learn from failures, and persevere.

6. Lead by Example: Be a role model by demonstrating the qualities and values that you hope to instill in your mentees.

7. Stay Connected: Maintain an ongoing relationship with your mentees. Offer support and guidance as they progress in their entrepreneurial journeys.

The Impact of Your Legacy

Nurturing the next generation of entrepreneurs through mentorship is a meaningful way to leave a positive impact. It extends your influence beyond your business success, contributing to the growth and development of future entrepreneurs and the broader entrepreneurial community.

Your legacy as a mindful entrepreneur is not only the businesses you've built but also the people you've inspired, the values you've upheld, and the positive impact you've made on the world. In this chapter, we celebrate the potential for your legacy to shape the future of entrepreneurship and make a lasting difference.

# 12

# Conclusion - The Endless Journey of Mindful Entrepreneurship

As we conclude this exploration of mindful entrepreneurship, it's important to recognize that the journey is ongoing and ever-evolving. Mindfulness is not a destination but a way of life, and its application in entrepreneurship is a dynamic process that continually adapts to new challenges and opportunities. In this final chapter, we reflect on the key lessons and principles we've explored and offer some parting thoughts as you continue your mindful entrepreneurial journey.

The Mindful Entrepreneurship Journey Revisited

Throughout this book, we've covered a wide range of topics, including:

- Mindful Leadership: The foundation of mindful entrepreneurship begins with your leadership style. By leading with authenticity, empathy, and a focus on well-being, you set the tone for your business and your team.

- Mindful Decision-Making: We've explored how mindfulness can enhance your decision-making process, helping you navigate the complexities of entrepreneurship with clarity and confidence.

- Work-Life Integration: The concept of work-life integration encourages you to find a harmonious balance between your personal and professional life, fostering well-being and sustainability.

- Resilience and Mindfulness: Resilience is a key quality for entrepreneurs, and mindfulness is a powerful tool to help you thrive in the face of adversity.

- Building a Purpose-Driven Business: Mindfulness can guide you in creating a business that aligns with your values and contributes to a better world.

- Mindful Growth and Scaling: The balance between expansion and well-being is critical in the process of growing your business.

- Mindful Adaptation and Innovation: As an entrepreneur, you must embrace change and innovate to navigate the evolving landscape of business.

- Mindful Success: The concept of mindful success emphasizes a holistic approach to achievement that balances well-being, values, and personal growth with financial success.

- A Mindful Entrepreneur's Legacy: As a successful entrepreneur, you have the opportunity to leave a meaningful legacy by nurturing the next generation of entrepreneurs through mentorship.

The Ongoing Journey

As you reflect on the principles and practices of mindful entrepreneurship, remember that the journey never truly ends. It's a continuous process of growth, self-discovery, and adaptation. The principles of mindfulness can be applied to every aspect of your entrepreneurial life, and as you face new

# CONCLUSION - THE ENDLESS JOURNEY OF MINDFUL ENTREPRENEURSHIP

challenges and opportunities, you'll find fresh ways to integrate mindfulness into your journey.

Your Unique Path

Your path as a mindful entrepreneur is unique to you, shaped by your values, experiences, and aspirations. Embrace your individuality and the opportunities that arise as you continue to build your business and make a positive impact on the world.

Parting Thoughts

Mindful entrepreneurship is a powerful approach to business that aligns your passion and purpose with the pursuit of success. It emphasizes well-being, values, and a positive impact on the world. As you navigate the entrepreneurial journey, keep these parting thoughts in mind:

1. Embrace Change: Change is a constant in entrepreneurship. Embrace it as an opportunity for growth, innovation, and adaptation.

2. Prioritize Well-Being: Your well-being is paramount. A healthy and balanced you is more equipped to lead your business to success.

3. Nurture Your Values: Stay true to your values and purpose. Let them guide your decisions and actions.

4. Celebrate Success: Success is a journey, not a destination. Celebrate your achievements, both big and small, along the way.

5. Pay It Forward: As you achieve success, consider how you can mentor and support the next generation of entrepreneurs, leaving a lasting legacy of positive impact.

6. Stay Mindful: Continue your mindfulness practice and keep its principles at the forefront of your entrepreneurial journey. Mindfulness is a lifelong pursuit.

The journey of mindful entrepreneurship is an enriching one, filled with challenges, triumphs, and the opportunity to make a meaningful impact on the world. As you move forward, remember that success is not only about what you achieve but how you achieve it—mindfully, purposefully, and in harmony with your values.

Summary:

"The Mindful Entrepreneur: Balance in a Hectic World" is a comprehensive exploration of how mindfulness can be applied to various aspects of entrepreneurship. The book is divided into twelve chapters, each addressing different facets of mindful entrepreneurship. Here is a brief summary of the key themes and principles discussed in each chapter:

1. Chapter 1: The Mindful Entrepreneur's Mindset: The book begins by introducing the concept of mindful entrepreneurship and the importance of cultivating a mindful mindset to navigate the challenges of the entrepreneurial journey.

2. Chapter 2: Mindful Leadership: This chapter focuses on the role of mindfulness in leadership, emphasizing authenticity, empathy, and well-being as essential qualities for effective leadership.

3. Chapter 3: Mindful Decision-Making: Mindfulness is explored as a tool for making more informed and grounded decisions, especially in the face of uncertainty.

4. Chapter 4: Work-Life Integration: The concept of work-life integration is introduced, highlighting the benefits of balancing personal and professional

## CONCLUSION - THE ENDLESS JOURNEY OF MINDFUL ENTREPRENEURSHIP

life through mindfulness.

5. Chapter 5: Work-Life Integration: A Mindful Approach to Balance: This chapter delves deeper into the practical application of mindfulness for work-life integration, providing tips and strategies.

6. Chapter 6: Resilience and Mindfulness: Resilience, an essential trait for entrepreneurs, is examined in the context of mindfulness, emphasizing the importance of adaptability and emotional regulation.

7. Chapter 7: Building a Purpose-Driven Business: The book explores the idea of creating a business with a meaningful purpose, driven by values and a commitment to making a positive impact on society.

8. Chapter 8: Mindful Growth and Scaling: This chapter addresses the challenges and opportunities of scaling a business mindfully, ensuring alignment with values and sustainability.

9. Chapter 9: Mindful Adaptation and Innovation: Mindfulness is presented as a powerful tool for navigating change, fostering resilience, and encouraging creative problem-solving.

10. Chapter 10: Mindful Success: Mindful success is defined as achieving success while maintaining well-being, values, and balance, and practical steps are provided for its realization.

11. Chapter 11: A Mindful Entrepreneur's Legacy: Leaving a lasting legacy as a mindful entrepreneur is explored through mentorship and support for the next generation of entrepreneurs.

12. Chapter 12: Conclusion - The Endless Journey of Mindful Entrepreneurship: The final chapter emphasizes that the journey of mindful entrepreneurship is ongoing, never truly ending. It encourages entrepreneurs to embrace

change, prioritize well-being, nurture their values, and celebrate success while staying true to their mindful principles.

The book's overarching message is that mindful entrepreneurship offers a holistic and balanced approach to business, where success is not only about financial achievements but also about well-being, values, and making a positive impact on the world. The book underscores the importance of mindfulness as a lifelong pursuit that continually evolves to address new challenges and opportunities.

www.ingramcontent.com/pod-product-compliance
Lightning Source LLC
LaVergne TN
LVHW010437070526
838199LV00066B/6051